Courageous Kids

IDA LEWIS GUARDS THE SHORE

Courageous Kid of the Atlantic

by Jessica Gunderson
illustrated by Nadia Hsieh

Consultant:
Richard Bell,
Associate Professor of History,
University of Maryland

CAPSTONE PRESS
a capstone imprint

Graphic Library is published by Capstone Press, an imprint of Capstone.
1710 Roe Crest Drive, North Mankato, Minnesota 56003
www.capstonepub.com

Library of Congress Cataloging-in-Publication Data

Names: Gunderson, Jessica, author.
Title: Ida Lewis guards the shore : courageous kid of the Atlantic / Jessica Gunderson.
Description: North Mankato, Minnesota : Capstone Press, [2021] | Series: Courageous kids | Includes bibliographical references and index. | Audience: Ages 8–11 | Audience: Grades 4-6 | Summary: "Ida Lewis spent a lifetime on the water, starting when her family moved to the island of Lime Rock in 1857 for her father's job as lighthouse keeper. By age 15, Ida was the best swimmer in Newport, Rhode Island. And when her father suffers a stroke, Ida herself takes over as keeper of the lighthouse. But guarding the shore also means guarding the water. And when Ida spots four local boys in danger on the water, she knows she must take action, the boys' lives depend on it"—Provided by publisher.
Identifiers: LCCN 2020003300 (print) | LCCN 2020003301 (ebook) | ISBN 9781496685056 (hardcover) | ISBN 9781496688064 (paperback) | ISBN 9781496685094 (pdf)
Subjects: LCSH: Lewis, Ida, 1842-1911—Juvenile literature. | Women lighthouse keepers—Rhode Island—Newport—Biography—Juvenile literature. | Women heroes—Rhode Island—Newport—Biography—Juvenile literature. | Newport (R.I.)—Biography—Juvenile literature. | Lifesaving—Rhode Island—Newport—History—Juvenile literature. | Ida Lewis Rock Light (R.I.)—History—Juvenile literature.
Classification: LCC VK1140.L48 G86 2021 (print) | LCC VK1140.L48 (ebook) | DDC 387.1/55092 [B]—dc23
LC record available at https://lccn.loc.gov/2020003300
LC ebook record available at https://lccn.loc.gov/2020003301

EDITOR
Alison Deering

ART DIRECTOR
Nathan Gassman

DESIGNER
Ted Williams

MEDIA RESEARCHER
Morgan Walters

PRODUCTION SPECIALIST
Laura Manthe

Printed in the United States 5205

TABLE OF CONTENTS

KEEPERS OF THE LIGHT
For hundreds of years, lighthouses have been fixtures along the coastline. They have warned sailors about the presence of rocks, sandbars, or shorelines. They've helped ships steer clear of these locations and avoid wrecking or running aground.

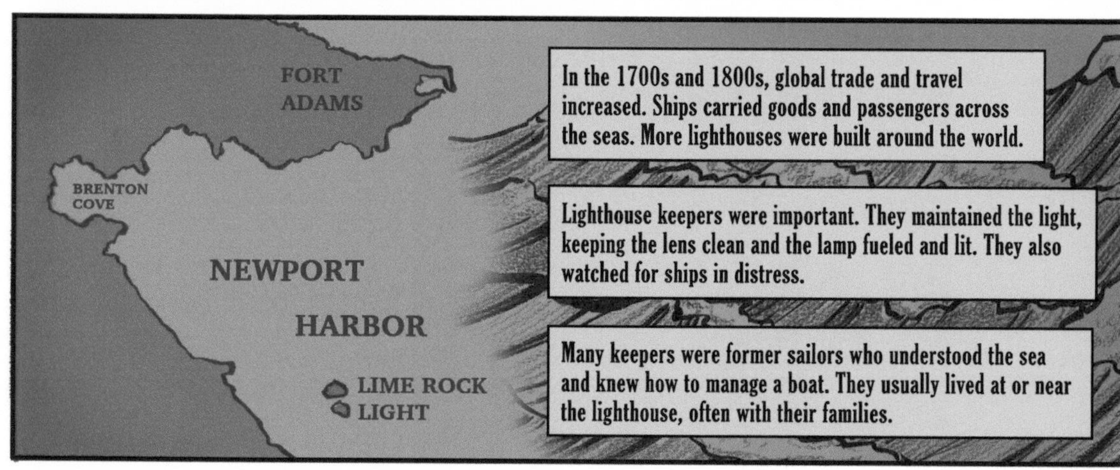
FORT ADAMS
BRENTON COVE
NEWPORT HARBOR
LIME ROCK LIGHT
In the 1700s and 1800s, global trade and travel increased. Ships carried goods and passengers across the seas. More lighthouses were built around the world.
Lighthouse keepers were important. They maintained the light, keeping the lens clean and the lamp fueled and lit. They also watched for ships in distress.
Many keepers were former sailors who understood the sea and knew how to manage a boat. They usually lived at or near the lighthouse, often with their families.

One of those keepers was Captain Hosea Lewis of Newport, Rhode Island. In the 1850s, Newport was a bustling port on the Atlantic Ocean. Lightships—boats that held a burning light—floated in the harbor to help guide boats.
Makeshift beacons, often bonfires, were placed along shore as well. But these beacons could be mimicked by pirates who aimed to lure boats. With all its activity, Newport Harbor needed a permanent lighthouse.

In 1854, construction began on a lighthouse on Lime Rock, a small limestone island in the harbor. Later that year, Captain Lewis was appointed keeper of the light.
For two years, the Lewis family remained in their home in Newport. Hosea rowed a small boat 220 yards to Lime Rock to tend the light. His oldest daughter, 12-year-old Ida, loved to swim and row. She often accompanied her father.
Have you ever seen ships in distress out there, Father?
Not yet. But if I do, it's my duty to come to their aid.
I would do the same. Even though I'm just a little girl!
Hosea made the trip to the lighthouse twice a day. Then, in August 1856, he received good news. . . .

Congress has approved funding to build a house for us on Lime Rock!

Oh, Father, that's wonderful! Life will be so much easier.

We'll no longer have to row from Newport to Lime Rock in the rain. . . .

. . . or the snow.

And I can help you clean the light every day.
Keep polishing! The cleaner the lens, the farther the light carries.
Together we can keep it burning.
Just a little more kerosene, and then we'll light the wick.
And keep sailors and ships safe! That's the light keeper's duty.

In June 1857, the Lewis family moved to Lime Rock. The family was happy in their new home. Ida played with her siblings and helped her father tend the light. She loved being close to the water.
But four months later . . .
Hosea!
What happened, Mother?
I don't know. He can't move! Quick, row to Newport and fetch the doctor!
Do you think he'll live, Doctor?
I won't know until I see him.
It seems he's had a stroke. Patients usually recover, although it takes time.
Ida, I can no longer tend the light. And your mother is busy with the little ones . . .
I can do it, Father. I remember everything you taught me.

With her father still recovering, Ida took over at Lime Rock Lighthouse. Every dusk and dawn, she tended the light.
She climbed the stairs of the tower, cleaned the lens, and lit the lamp.
And every day, she rowed her younger siblings to the mainland to attend school. Ida soon became strong and skilled at handling the rowboat.
It's not fair. Why don't *you* have to go to school?
I'm already done with school!
You're such a strong rower, Ida. Stronger than I ever was! I never worry when the kids are with you.
But remember what I taught you. If anyone falls in . . .
I know, Father. Bring them back into the boat by the stern. Otherwise the boat will tip.
You learn well, Ida.

DANGER ON THE WATER
September 4, 1858
It's a beautiful day, isn't it?
Yes, but . . .
It's one of those days that can change quickly.
I better go swimming while I can, then!
Wonder where they're going . . .
Do you know them? They look your age.
Probably out to one of the islands for a picnic. Kids from school always used do that.

It's Sam Powell and his friends Lance, Ted, and Smith. Kids from the private school. I doubt they know me, though.
A few hours later, Ida went about her duties.
It'll be dark early. I should light the lamp soon.
As she was preparing to ready the lamp, Ida caught sight of movement in the harbor.
Those boys are still out there? They'd better hurry in before dark. . . .

Let's lower the sail and float to the wharf.
Don't fall in, Ted!
Oh no, I'm gonna fall!
Those boys are so rowdy!
Watch this, boys!
No! Don't climb the mast!

Whoa!
Ahhhh!
SPLASH!
SPLASH!

They're drowning!
I have to help them!
HELP!
Oh thank heavens!
I have to hurry.
This weather is
getting worse.
NNNNPH!
UNNN!

I'm coming!
HELP! Help us!

I can't hold on!
GRGL

ROWING TO THE RESCUE
Ida rowed as fast as she could. It took all her strength to battle the churning water and punishing winds.
Hang tight! I'm coming!
Drat this wind!
NNNNPH! UNNN!
Captain Lewis watched Ida row toward the boys. He was unable to help, but he had faith in his strong, capable daughter.

You can save them, Ida. I know you can.
I need to hurry. Every second counts!
My legs . . . so heavy . . .
Where's Sam?
I-I can't . . . keep on . . .

UNDERWATER
Help! Help me! I'm over here!
Swim, Sam! Get to the boat.
Is that a . . . rescue boat?
Oh no. It's just a girl.
I hope she's strong enough to help us!

This wind is exhausting. But I've rowed in worse.
I know I can do it.
Ida churned through the water, rowing as fast as she could toward the stranded boys.
Hurry, miss! We can't tread water for much longer!
I hope she remembers what I told her. . . .

Come around the stern side . . .
No! Don't grab there or the boat will tip!
Ohhh . . . so cold . . .
One at a time!
Just one more to save . . .
Hold on!

Are we really still alive?
I think so.
Lance! Where are you?
We can't let him go under!
Lance? Answer us!

There he is!
Help me!
Hold tight!
Come on, pull harder!
Uhhn!

Is everyone here? Everyone okay?
Yes. We're all here.
Ida set off toward Lime Rock.
Do you want *me* to row?
I've got it. Thanks.
Miss, Sam's not breathing!
GASP!

NEAR DEATH
I'm trying to find his pulse!
Please no, he can't be dead. . . .
He's still breathing. But we need to get him ashore—quickly! Hand me my oars!
I need to row faster than ever before. Sam's life depends on it.
Wow! You can really row.
I've had a lot of practice.

SCCRRRAPE!
We made it!
Land! At last.
We need to get Sam inside! Quickly!
Go on inside. I'll be in . . .
. . . as soon as I light the lamp.
Ida completed her duties as keeper, lighting the lamp to guide ships at sea. Then she returned to the Lewis kitchen, where the boys were waiting for her.
I guess he does know my name.
Ida, thank you. You saved my life!
No problem. It's my duty as a lighthouse keeper.

The rescue of the four boys wasn't Ida's last. On March 29, 1869, when Ida was 27, she made another daring save. . . .
Quite a storm out there!
Yes. The last time I looked, snow was falling along with the rain.
Ida, run quick! A boat has capsized!
I must hurry!
There!
Who would be out during this storm?
Ida, wait! It's dangerous.
There's no time to spare!
Your coat!
Help! Anyone out there?
We're drowning!
You won't drown. Not if I can help it.

Thought we were gonna die out here!
Much obliged, ma'am. You risked your life to save us.
I'm a lighthouse keeper. I'm always on watch.
And I can row through any storm!
Word soon spread about Ida's dramatic rescue of the soldiers.
Ida Lewis? I'm from the *New-York Tribune*.
New York?
Was this your first rescue?
No. Once, when I was 16, I saw four boys in the water. . . .

THE BRAVEST WOMAN IN AMERICA
After the *New-York Tribune* article appeared, Ida Lewis was swept into fame. On July 4, 1869, a parade was held in her honor. More than 4,000 people flooded Newport, Rhode Island, for a chance to glimpse the young heroine.
Ida was presented with a shiny new rowboat called the *Rescue*. She also received flags to fly on her rowboat.
Ida's father, Hosea Lewis, died in 1872. Ida and her mother, Zoradia, continued to share lighthouse duties. Zoradia, however, spent much of her time caring for her younger daughter, Hattie, who had a lung condition. That meant much of the work fell to Ida.
During her time at Lime Rock Lighthouse, Ida Lewis saved at least 18 lives, although the actual number may be as many as 25.
One of Ida's most daring rescues took place in February 1881. The waters of the harbor were frozen. From the kitchen window, Ida saw two men making their way across the ice. Then, the ice broke, and the men fell into the freezing water. Ida raced outside, grabbed a clothesline, and threw it to the men to haul them ashore.
For this rescue, she was awarded the Gold Lifesaving Medal from the U.S. government. She was the first woman to receive the award. She became known as the "bravest woman in America."
In 1879, Ida was named the official keeper of Lime Rock Lighthouse. It was the moment she'd been waiting for.

Ida Lewis lived a long life and died in 1911, at the age of 69. In 1924, the Rhode Island legislature officially changed the name of Lime Rock Lighthouse to Ida Lewis Rock Lighthouse.
Today, the lighthouse is the clubhouse for the Ida Lewis Yacht Club. In 2018, a road at Arlington National Cemetery was named after Ida—the first to be named after a woman.

GLOSSARY

capsize (KAP-syz)—to tip over in the water

kerosene (KER-uh-seen)—a thin, colorless fuel that is made from petroleum

lightship (LAYHT-ship)—a ship equipped with a brilliant light and moored at a place dangerous to navigation

mainland (MAIN-land)—a continent or the largest part of a continent as distinguished from an offshore island or islands

makeshift (MEYK-shift)—serving as a temporary substitute

mariners (MAR-uh-nerz)—people who navigate or assist in navigating a ship

mast (MAST)—a tall pole on a ship's/boat's deck that holds its sails

stern (STERN)—the back half of a ship

stroke (STROHK)—a medical condition that occurs when a blocked blood vessel stops oxygen from reaching the brain

READ MORE

Roop, Connie and Peter Roop. *The Stormy Adventure of Abbie Burgess, Lighthouse Keeper.* Minneapolis: Lerner Publishing, 2016.

Tougias, Michael J. *Into the Blizzard: Heroism at Sea During the Great Blizzard of 1978.* New York: Henry Holt, 2019.

Welldon, Christine. *My House is a Lighthouse: Stories of Lighthouses and Their Keepers.* Halifax, Nova Scotia: Nimbus Publishing, 2019.

INTERNET SITES

Rhode Island Lighthouse History
http://www.rhodeislandlighthousehistory.info/lime_rock_lighthouse.html

Women & the Sea—The Mariners' Museum
https://www.marinersmuseum.org/sites/micro/women/lighthouse/ida.htm

Ida Lewis Rock Lighthouse
https://www.lighthousefriends.com/light.asp?ID=398

INDEX

Plants Love Compost

The compost bin

This is our compost bin.
Our compost bin
is in our garden.

3

Kitchen rubbish

We put kitchen **rubbish**
into our compost bin.
This can go
in our compost bin.

This can not go
in our compost bin.

Garden rubbish

We put garden rubbish
into our compost bin.
This can go
in our compost bin.

This can not go

in our compost bin.

My little fork

This is my little **fork**.

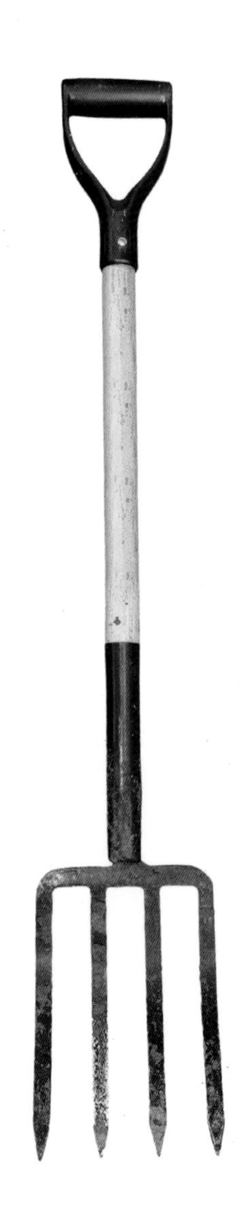

I dig in the compost bin with my little fork.

Worms

Can you see
the little worms?
The little worms
like the compost.

11

The compost

Look at the compost.

The compost is brown.

The compost is like **soil**.

Our garden

We will put the compost
into our garden.
The compost will
help our garden grow.

Glossary

fork

rubbish

soil